The Anatomy of Murder

Copyright © 2024 by Patrick Morgan
All rights reserved. No part of this book may be reproduced in any manner whatsoever without written permission except in the case of brief quotations embodied in critical articles and reviews.
First Printing, 2024

The Anatomy of Murder

Patrick Morgan

CONTENTS

1. Introduction to Murder Methods — 1
2. Historical Murder Methods — 9
3. Psychological Profiles of Murderers — 21
4. Forensic Science in Murder Cases — 31
5. Infamous Serial Killers and Their Techniques — 41
6. Cultural Perspectives on Murder Methods — 53
7. Legal Implications of Various Murder Methods — 65

8 Murder Methods in True Crime Documentaries 75

9 Analysis of Unsolved Murder Cases 85

10 Ethical Considerations in Studying Murder Methods 95

11 Conclusion 105

1

Introduction to Murder Methods

Defining Murder: An Overview

Murder, the unlawful killing of another human being with malice aforethought, encompasses a range of motivations, methods, and implications that have fascinated and horrified society throughout history. This subchapter aims to define murder by examining its legal definitions, historical context, and the various classifications that have emerged over time. True crime enthusiasts often delve into the complexities of this crime, seeking to understand not only the act itself but also the psychological profiles of those who commit it and the societal responses that follow.

At its core, murder can be categorized into several types, including first-degree murder, second-degree murder, and manslaughter. First-degree murder involves premeditation, where the perpetrator plans the act beforehand, while second-degree murder lacks this planning but still demonstrates an intent to kill. Manslaughter, often seen as a lesser charge, can arise from a sudden emotional disturbance, reflecting a significant difference in legal consequences. By exploring these classifications, true crime enthusiasts can better appreciate the nuances that differentiate various murder cases and their corresponding legal outcomes.

Historical perspectives on murder reveal significant shifts in societal attitudes and legal frameworks over time. In ancient civilizations, murder was often regarded through the lens of honor and retribution, with community-driven justice systems in place. The introduction of formal legal codes, such as the Code of Hammurabi, marked a pivotal change, emphasizing structured penalties and societal order. Understanding these historical contexts enriches the analysis of modern murder cases and the psychological factors that may drive individuals to commit such acts.

The psychological profiles of murderers are critical to understanding the motivations behind their actions. Many infamous serial killers, for instance, exhibit patterns of behavior that can be analyzed through various psychological theories. Factors such as childhood trauma, mental illness, and sociopathy often play pivotal roles in shaping their actions. True crime enthusiasts can gain insights into these profiles, exploring how forensic psychology contributes to both the investigation of cases and the prevention of future crimes.

Finally, the ethical considerations in studying murder methods cannot be overlooked. While the fascination with murder cases and their methodologies can lead to greater awareness and understanding, it also raises questions about the impact of true crime media on society. Sensationalism can undermine the gravity of these crimes and affect public perception of justice. By navigating these ethical dilemmas, true crime enthusiasts can engage in a more responsible exploration of murder, balancing the need for knowledge with respect for the victims and their families.

The Evolution of Murder Techniques

The evolution of murder techniques is a revealing reflection of societal changes, technological advancements, and psychological developments throughout history. In ancient times, methods of killing were often brutal and direct, relying on physical strength and weapons readily available in one's environment. The use of bladed instruments, blunt force, and eventually firearms marked the early landscape of murder, where the act itself was often a visceral demonstration of power, rage, or survival. These primitive methods were less about stealth and more about immediacy, as the killer's identity was frequently known to the victim, reflecting the communal nature of early societies.

As societies advanced, so too did the techniques employed by murderers. The rise of urbanization and the anonymity it provided led to a shift in the psychological profiles of murderers. In the 19th century, with the advent of industrialization, murderers began to adopt more calculated approaches, often relying on poisons or methods that minimized immediate detection. The infamous case of the "Angel of Death" exemplifies this transition, where the murderer used their position of trust in healthcare to commit heinous acts, showcasing how societal roles could be manipulated for sinister purposes. This period also saw the emergence of forensic science, which began to play a critical role in understanding and solving murder cases.

The 20th century brought about even more sophisticated methods, influenced by advancements in technology and a growing understanding of human psychology. Serial killers gained notoriety for their ability to evade capture, employing techniques that highlighted both their cunning and their understanding of law enforcement. Infamous figures like Ted Bundy and John Wayne Gacy developed distinct patterns that reflected not only their personal psychologies but also the cultural contexts of their crimes. Documentaries exploring these figures often emphasize the chilling normalcy of their lives juxtaposed with their brutal acts, providing insight into the dualities present in many murderers.

Cultural perspectives also played a significant role in shaping murder techniques. Different societies have varied in their moral interpretations and legal implications surrounding the act of murder. For instance, some cultures may have historically viewed certain forms of murder as acceptable under specific circumstances, such as honor killings or ritualistic sacrifices. These cultural lenses influence not only the methods chosen but also the societal reactions and legal frameworks established in response to such acts. Understanding these variations deepens the analysis of unsolved murder cases, as it encourages a broader examination of motives and societal norms.

Ethical considerations in studying murder methods have become increasingly important in contemporary discussions. The fascination with murder techniques, particularly in true crime media, raises questions about glorification versus education. While it is essential to analyze the psychological and forensic aspects of murder, it is equally crucial to approach the subject with sensitivity to the victims and their families. As true crime enthusiasts delve into the gritty details of historical and modern techniques, the responsibility lies in ensuring that the narrative does not overshadow the human cost of these violent acts. By maintaining this balance, the examination of murder techniques can foster a deeper understanding of both the dark corners of human behavior and the societal frameworks that enable such tragedies to occur.

2

Historical Murder Methods

Ancient Techniques: From Poison to Bludgeoning

Ancient societies developed a variety of murder techniques that reflected their environmental, cultural, and technological contexts. Among these methods, poisoning stands out as one of the most insidious and covert forms of homicide. The use of toxic substances dates back to antiquity, with historical records indicating that both the aristocracy and the common people utilized poisons for various nefarious purposes. Ancient Greek and Roman texts detail the usage of plant-based toxins, such as hemlock and belladonna, which were often employed in political assassinations and personal vendettas. The ability to deliver death discreetly appealed to those wishing to eliminate rivals without the overt violence that bludgeoning or stabbing would entail.

Bludgeoning, on the other hand, represents a more visceral and immediate approach to murder. From prehistoric times, the use of blunt instruments has been evidenced in archaeological findings, indicating that early humans employed whatever tools were at hand to inflict fatal injuries. This method of murder often left clear signs of struggle, making it a less subtle approach than poisoning. However, the psychological implications of bludgeoning can be profound; it requires a level of physical confrontation that can escalate emotions and reveal deeper, more primal instincts within the perpetrator. This reflects a stark contrast to the cold calculation associated with poisoning, showcasing the diverse motivations behind murderous acts.

The choice between poison and bludgeoning often reveals much about the psychological profiles of murderers. Those who resort to poison may exhibit traits of cunning and deceit, preferring to evade direct confrontation while orchestrating the demise of their target from a distance. In contrast, individuals who favor bludgeoning might display more impulsive or aggressive tendencies, engaging directly with their victims in a manner that can be both physically and emotionally charged. This dichotomy in methods raises important questions for forensic scientists and criminal psychologists as they analyze crime scenes and attempt to understand the motivations driving these acts of violence.

Cultural perspectives on murder methods also influence the prevalence and acceptance of certain techniques throughout history. In some societies, poisoning was viewed as a refined or honorable method of killing, particularly in the context of political intrigue. Conversely, bludgeoning has often been associated with barbarism and brutality, reflecting societal values surrounding honor, strength, and the nature of violence itself. These cultural attitudes not only shape individual behavior but also impact legal implications, as societies grapple with the morality and legality of various methods of murder. Understanding these cultural nuances can provide deeper insight into historical cases and the societal frameworks that shaped them.

The study of ancient murder techniques offers valuable lessons for modern true crime enthusiasts and scholars alike. By examining the historical context of poisoning and bludgeoning, enthusiasts can better appreciate the complex interplay between method, motive, and societal influence. Moreover, these insights can inform discussions on contemporary murder cases, including unsolved mysteries and infamous serial killers whose techniques may echo those of the past. As forensic science continues to evolve, the ethical considerations surrounding the study of murder methods also become increasingly pertinent, prompting ongoing dialogue about the implications of examining such dark chapters of human behavior.

Medieval Methods: The Art of Execution

Medieval methods of execution were not merely punitive measures; they were elaborate spectacles designed to convey the power of the state and the moral order of society. During this era, execution served multiple purposes: it was a deterrent, a form of justice, and a public display meant to reinforce societal norms. The techniques employed varied significantly across regions and cultures, influenced by local beliefs, legal systems, and the severity of the crimes committed. Understanding these methods provides valuable insights into not only the historical context of crime and punishment but also the psychological profiles of both the executed and the executioners.

One of the most notorious methods of execution in medieval Europe was hanging, which was often seen as a less brutal option compared to others. However, the method varied in its execution, with some hangings resulting in a slow death by strangulation if not properly conducted. In contrast, the infamous drawing and quartering of traitors involved a gruesome series of events designed to maximize suffering and public humiliation. This brutal method reflected societal attitudes toward treason, which was considered one of the most heinous offenses of the time. The psychological impact of such executions on both the public and the perpetrators reveals much about the cultural norms surrounding justice and morality during the medieval period.

Burning at the stake was another prominent execution method, particularly for those accused of witchcraft or heresy. This method was laden with symbolic meaning, representing the purification of the soul through fire and the eradication of evil from society. The choice of this method often stemmed from a desire to instill fear within the community, serving as a stark warning against deviating from established norms or beliefs. The social implications of such executions were profound, as they not only targeted individuals but also aimed to suppress entire communities. The psychological ramifications for those involved, from the accused to the spectators, were significant, contributing to a culture of fear that could influence behavior for generations.

The role of the executioner was equally complex, often straddling the line between a necessary evil and a figure of public scorn. Executioners were sometimes stigmatized, forced to live on the fringes of society due to the nature of their work. However, they also held a position of power and authority, tasked with enforcing the law and meting out justice. The psychological profiles of these individuals are particularly intriguing, as many executioners developed coping mechanisms to reconcile their roles with the moral implications of their duties. Some took pride in their work, viewing it as a vital service to society, while others struggled with the emotional toll of inflicting death.

As modern society reflects on these historical methods, the cultural perspectives on execution continue to evolve. The ethical considerations surrounding the study of such methods are critical, especially in the context of true crime narratives and documentaries that seek to engage audiences with these grim topics. By analyzing the legal implications, societal reactions, and psychological profiles associated with medieval executions, enthusiasts of true crime can gain a deeper understanding of the motivations behind these practices and their lasting impact on contemporary views of justice and morality. The study of medieval execution methods not only reveals the darker aspects of human nature but also serves as a cautionary tale about the consequences of societal fear and the quest for control.

Modern Advances: Technology and Murder

The intersection of technology and murder has evolved dramatically in recent years, reshaping the landscape of criminal investigation and the methods employed by perpetrators. With the advent of digital tools, murderers now have access to sophisticated means that enhance their ability to execute and cover up their crimes. This includes everything from the use of the internet for planning and communication to the manipulation of smart devices that can provide alibis or record evidence. The increasing reliance on technology not only changes the methods of murder but also complicates the psychological profiles of offenders, who may feel emboldened by the anonymity that the digital world offers.

Forensic science has also seen revolutionary advances that aid in solving murder cases. Techniques such as DNA analysis, digital forensics, and advanced ballistics have transformed the way evidence is collected and interpreted. In the past, investigators often relied on circumstantial evidence or witness testimonies, which could be unreliable. Today, forensic scientists can analyze minute traces of DNA left at a crime scene, sometimes leading to breakthroughs years after the crime was committed. This scientific rigor not only helps to convict the guilty but also exonerates the innocent, highlighting the ethical considerations that arise in the realm of justice.

The rise of cybercrime has introduced new murder methods that exploit technology. For instance, the use of poison via digital means, such as tampering with medical devices or contaminating food delivery systems, presents a chilling new frontier for murderers. Serial killers have adapted their techniques in response to advances in technology, often using social media to stalk victims or lure them into traps. This evolution underscores the importance of understanding not only the historical context of murder methods but also how they change in response to societal advancements.

Cultural perspectives on murder methods vary significantly, influenced by the technology prevalent in different societies. In some cultures, the use of technology in committing murder is viewed through a lens of innovation, while in others, it raises ethical concerns about the detachment it creates between the perpetrator and the act itself. Documentaries and media portrayals of murder cases often emphasize these cultural narratives, exploring how technology shapes public perception and fear. True crime enthusiasts are drawn to these stories, seeking to understand the complexities of human behavior in the context of modern advancements.

Legal implications surrounding murder methods have also become more intricate with technological advancements. Legislatures have struggled to keep pace with the rapid evolution of crime, often lagging behind in updating laws to address new forms of murder. This has led to challenges in prosecuting offenders who utilize technology to commit crimes, as traditional legal frameworks may not adequately cover these cases. The discussion of these legal limitations is essential for true crime enthusiasts, as it provides insight into the systemic issues within the criminal justice system and highlights the ongoing need for reform in light of changing murder methodologies.

3

Psychological Profiles of Murderers

The Mind of a Killer: Psychological Theories

The exploration of the psychological underpinnings of murderers has long captivated true crime enthusiasts, offering insight into the minds that commit such heinous acts. Various psychological theories attempt to explain the motivations and behaviors of killers, ranging from biological predispositions to environmental influences. Theories such as the psychopathology model suggest that certain mental disorders may predispose individuals to violence, while the social learning theory posits that exposure to violent behavior can shape an individual's propensity for aggression. By examining these frameworks, we can gain a deeper understanding of the complexities involved in the psychology of murder.

One prominent theory is the psychodynamic perspective, which emphasizes the influence of unconscious motivations and early childhood experiences on behavior. Sigmund Freud's concepts of the id, ego, and superego are often invoked to explain the internal conflicts that may lead an individual to commit murder. This perspective suggests that unresolved traumas or deep-seated desires can manifest in violent actions. Analyzing infamous cases, such as that of Ed Gein, reveals how early familial relationships and psychological disturbances can intertwine, resulting in the emergence of a killer.

Another significant psychological framework is the trait theory, which focuses on identifying specific personality traits associated with violent behavior. Traits such as impulsivity, aggression, and a lack of empathy are often highlighted in the profiles of serial killers. Research has shown that many notorious murderers exhibit elevated levels of traits associated with psychopathy, which can lead to a detachment from moral consequences. Understanding these traits not only aids in profiling known killers but also assists law enforcement in predicting potential violent behaviors in individuals who display similar characteristics.

Cultural perspectives also play a crucial role in shaping the psychology of murderers. Different societies have varying thresholds for violence and diverse social norms that can influence an individual's actions. For instance, cultures that glorify violence or have a history of conflict may produce individuals more likely to commit murder. Additionally, societal factors such as poverty, abuse, and exposure to crime can contribute to the development of violent tendencies. Recognizing these cultural influences is vital for a comprehensive understanding of murder methods and the psychological profiles of those who engage in them.

Finally, the ethical implications of studying the psychology of murderers cannot be overlooked.

While profiling and understanding these individuals can inform preventive measures and legal strategies, it also raises questions about the potential for stigmatization and the portrayal of mental illness in media. True crime enthusiasts must navigate the fine line between curiosity and sensitivity, ensuring that the study of these psychological theories serves a purpose beyond mere fascination. By fostering a responsible discourse around the psychology of murder, we can contribute to a more nuanced understanding of this dark aspect of human behavior.

Motives Behind Murder: A Comprehensive Analysis

Motives behind murder are as varied and complex as the individuals who commit these heinous acts. Understanding these motives is crucial for true crime enthusiasts, as they provide insight into the psychological and sociocultural factors that drive individuals to kill. Common motivations include passion, financial gain, revenge, and psychological gratification. Each of these motives can manifest in different ways, leading to distinct murder methods that reflect the perpetrator's intent and emotional state. By examining these motives, enthusiasts can better appreciate the intricacies of murder and the factors that influence criminal behavior.

Passion-driven murders often arise from intense emotional states, such as jealousy or betrayal. These crimes are typically impulsive, occurring in the heat of the moment, and often involve intimate partners or close acquaintances. The methods employed in these cases can be brutal and personal, reflecting the emotional turmoil of the perpetrator. Historical examples, such as the infamous case of Othello, demonstrate how jealousy can lead to tragic outcomes. Understanding these motives helps enthusiasts recognize the psychological underpinnings of such crimes and the broader implications for interpersonal relationships.

Financial motives for murder can stem from greed, desperation, or the desire for power. These calculations often lead to premeditated acts, where the murderer meticulously plans the crime to maximize gain while minimizing the risk of capture. Infamous serial killers like Harold Shipman and their methods illustrate how financial incentives can drive individuals to commit murder. True crime enthusiasts can delve into case studies that reveal the chilling rationalizations behind these acts and the forensic evidence that often unravels such elaborate schemes, highlighting the intersection of financial motives and criminal techniques.

Revenge is another potent motive, often resulting from perceived wrongs or injustices. This motive can lead to elaborate planning and a desire for psychological satisfaction, making the act of murder a form of retribution. Historical contexts, such as vendettas in organized crime or familial disputes, shed light on how cultural attitudes towards revenge can shape murder methods. Analyzing these cases allows enthusiasts to explore the ethical considerations surrounding revenge killings and the societal norms that may influence an individual's decision to resort to murder.

Lastly, psychological gratification can drive individuals to kill for reasons that may not be immediately apparent. Serial killers often exhibit this motive, deriving pleasure or excitement from the act of murder itself. The case studies of notorious killers such as Ted Bundy or Jeffrey Dahmer reveal the chilling interplay between psychological disorders and criminal behavior. Exploring the psychological profiles of these individuals not only fascinates true crime enthusiasts but also raises important questions about the nature of evil and the limits of empathy in understanding such profound moral transgressions. By comprehensively analyzing the motives behind murder, enthusiasts gain deeper insights into the complexities of criminal behavior and the societal implications that arise from these tragic events.

Case Studies: Infamous Murderers and Their Profiles

The study of infamous murderers provides a crucial window into the psychological underpinnings of violent crime, revealing not only the methods they employed but also the societal factors that shaped their actions. Serial killers, in particular, often exhibit a disturbing pattern of behavior that can be traced through their early lives, influencing their motivations and the methods they choose for their crimes. For instance, examining the life of Ted Bundy highlights the intersection of charm and manipulation. His ability to appear trustworthy allowed him to lure victims, showcasing a psychological profile that combined narcissism and antisocial behavior, which is often a hallmark of serial killers.

Another notable case is that of Jack the Ripper, whose identity remains one of the most infamous mysteries in criminal history. The methods employed by this unidentified murderer were particularly gruesome, involving precise surgical techniques that suggested a background in medicine or anatomy. This case is not only significant for its brutal nature but also for the cultural impact it had on society at the time, reflecting Victorian fears surrounding urban crime and the vulnerability of women. The lack of forensic science tools available in the late 19th century further complicates the investigation, making it a prime example of how legal implications and investigative techniques have evolved since then.

The psychological profiles of murderers like Jeffrey Dahmer reveal a complex interplay of mental illness and environmental factors. Dahmer's crimes, which included not only murder but also acts of necrophilia and cannibalism, stemmed from deep-seated issues related to his upbringing and sexuality. His case illustrates the importance of understanding the psychological nuances that drive individuals to commit heinous acts. Forensic psychology plays a vital role in dissecting these profiles, providing insight into the mindset of individuals who engage in such extreme violence and helping law enforcement develop strategies for prevention and intervention.

Cultural perspectives on murder methods also come into play when examining infamous figures like Aileen Wuornos. Her story reflects societal failures, highlighting issues such as poverty, gender-based violence, and the criminal justice system's treatment of women. Wuornos's murders were framed within a narrative of self-defense against male violence, challenging conventional views on female criminals. Her case raises ethical considerations regarding the portrayal of murderers in media and the potential influence of sensationalism on public perception, urging true crime enthusiasts to critically analyze narratives surrounding female killers.

Finally, the exploration of unsolved murder cases, such as the Zodiac Killer, underscores the ongoing challenges faced by law enforcement and the advancements in forensic science that continue to shape criminal investigations. The Zodiac Killer's cryptic letters and taunting messages have captivated both the public and investigators for decades, illustrating how the methods and motivations of murderers can create enduring mysteries. This case exemplifies the need for continued research and analysis in the field of true crime, as evolving forensic techniques may one day provide answers to questions that have lingered for generations. The complexities of these cases not only intrigue true crime enthusiasts but also emphasize the importance of understanding the broader implications of murder in society.

4

Forensic Science in Murder Cases

The Role of Forensics: From Crime Scene to Courtroom

The role of forensics in the criminal justice system is pivotal, bridging the gap between the chaotic reality of a crime scene and the structured environment of a courtroom. Forensic science encompasses a broad range of techniques, from DNA analysis to ballistics, each contributing crucial evidence that aids in solving murders. In the context of historical murder methods, forensic advancements have transformed how investigators approach crime scenes, allowing them to uncover details that were once beyond reach. This evolution not only enhances the accuracy of investigations but also serves to educate true crime enthusiasts about the methodologies that have shaped our understanding of criminal behavior.

At a crime scene, the initial response is critical. First responders must secure the area to prevent contamination, allowing forensic experts to meticulously document the scene. This involves taking photographs, sketching layouts, and collecting physical evidence such as fingerprints, fibers, and biological samples. Each piece of evidence serves as a silent witness, telling a story that, when pieced together, can lead to the identification of a perpetrator. For true crime enthusiasts, appreciating the meticulous nature of these processes sheds light on the complexities involved in solving murders and the importance of thoroughness in forensic investigations.

The transition from crime scene to courtroom hinges on the effective presentation of forensic evidence. Forensic experts often serve as key witnesses, translating complex scientific findings into understandable terms for juries. This role is critical, particularly in cases involving historical murder methods where the context may be unfamiliar to modern audiences. By elucidating how specific techniques, such as poison analysis or tool mark identification, played a role in the crime, forensic professionals help jurors grasp the significance of the evidence presented. This understanding is vital for the jury's decision-making process, emphasizing the need for clarity and precision in forensic testimony.

Moreover, the psychological profiles of murderers often intertwine with forensic evidence, providing insight into their motives and methods. Forensic psychologists work alongside investigators to analyze behavior patterns, offering perspectives that can influence both the investigation and the prosecution's strategy in court. Understanding the psychological underpinnings of a crime can illuminate the reasoning behind certain murder methods, enriching the narrative for true crime enthusiasts who seek to comprehend the complexities of human behavior in relation to violence and criminality.

Finally, as forensic science continues to evolve, ethical considerations arise regarding its application in murder cases. Discussions around the use of forensic evidence often touch on issues such as privacy, the potential for bias, and the implications of relying on technology in investigations. For true crime enthusiasts, exploring these ethical dimensions not only deepens their understanding of forensic science but also encourages critical thinking about the broader legal implications of various murder methods. As we reflect on the role of forensics from the crime scene to the courtroom, it becomes clear that this discipline is not just about solving crimes; it is a vital part of the ongoing dialogue about justice, morality, and the human condition.

Advances in Forensic Technology

Advances in forensic technology have revolutionized the field of criminal investigation, particularly in murder cases. With the advent of DNA analysis, investigators can now link suspects to crime scenes with unprecedented accuracy. This technology allows for the identification of individuals based on biological samples left behind, such as hair, blood, or skin cells. The ability to analyze trace evidence has not only aided in solving cold cases but has also exonerated individuals wrongfully convicted of murder. As true crime enthusiasts, understanding these advancements provides insight into how forensic science has evolved and its impact on historical and contemporary murder investigations.

Another significant advancement in forensic technology is the development of digital forensics. As crime increasingly intersects with technology, digital evidence has become crucial in solving murder cases. Investigators can now retrieve deleted files, track online activities, and analyze social media interactions to build psychological profiles of murderers. This technological leap has enhanced the ability to piece together the motives and methods behind infamous serial killers, allowing for a deeper understanding of their psychological makeup. True crime narratives often highlight the role of digital footprints in unraveling complex cases, showcasing how modern techniques are essential in the pursuit of justice.

Moreover, forensic anthropology has emerged as a vital tool in identifying victims and determining cause of death. By examining skeletal remains, forensic anthropologists can provide insights into the identity, age, sex, and even the lifestyle of deceased individuals. This discipline has proved invaluable in historical murder cases where remains have been discovered years after the crime occurred. The application of forensic anthropology not only aids in solving cases but also contributes to the broader cultural perspective on murder methods, as it sheds light on historical practices surrounding death and burial.

The integration of advanced imaging techniques, such as CT scans and 3D reconstruction, has further transformed forensic science. These technologies allow for non-invasive examinations of bodies and crime scenes, enabling investigators to visualize and analyze evidence without disturbing the original context. This approach has implications for legal proceedings, as it ensures that evidence is preserved in its most authentic state, potentially influencing the outcome of trials. True crime enthusiasts often find the visualization of such complex evidence fascinating, as it brings a new dimension to the narratives surrounding infamous murder cases.

Finally, ethical considerations in the study of murder methods have gained prominence alongside technological advancements. As forensic techniques become more sophisticated, the potential for misuse or overreach in investigations raises critical questions about privacy and consent. True crime enthusiasts must grapple with the implications of these technologies, recognizing the fine line between solving crimes and infringing on individual rights. As forensic science continues to evolve, it is essential to maintain a dialogue about the ethical responsibilities of investigators to ensure that advancements serve the pursuit of justice while respecting the dignity of victims and their families.

Notable Cases Solved by Forensic Evidence

Forensic evidence has played a pivotal role in solving numerous high-profile murder cases throughout history, often transforming the landscape of criminal justice. One of the most notable cases is that of the 1995 O.J. Simpson trial, where DNA evidence emerged as a cornerstone of the prosecution's case. The collection and analysis of blood samples, hair follicles, and other biological materials not only pointed to Simpson as the primary suspect but also sparked a national conversation about race, celebrity, and the legal system. Despite the compelling forensic evidence presented, the case ended in an acquittal, highlighting the complexities and occasional limitations of forensic science in the courtroom.

Another significant case is the 1996 murder of JonBenét Ramsey, a six-year-old beauty queen found dead in her family home in Boulder, Colorado. The investigation was marred by missteps and media frenzy, yet forensic techniques, including DNA analysis and the examination of a ransom note, provided critical insights. The presence of foreign DNA on JonBenét's body suggested an intruder might be responsible, challenging the initial focus on her family. This case illustrates the potential of forensic evidence to both clarify and complicate narratives surrounding murder, as well as the ethical considerations involved in public speculation.

The 2002 murder of Laci Peterson is another case where forensic science was instrumental. The discovery of her remains and those of her unborn child in San Francisco Bay led to a meticulous investigation. Forensic experts utilized various techniques, including entomology and ballistics, to establish a timeline and link her husband, Scott Peterson, to the crime. The case captivated the media and public, showcasing how forensic evidence can enhance the prosecution's narrative while simultaneously raising questions about the presumption of innocence and the influence of public opinion on legal proceedings.

In more recent times, the use of forensic genealogy in the Golden State Killer case exemplifies the evolving nature of forensic science. In 2018, investigators used DNA from crime scenes to create a familial link leading to Joseph DeAngelo, a former police officer. This breakthrough not only solved cases that had stymied detectives for decades but also raised discussions about privacy rights and ethical considerations in using genetic databases for criminal investigations. The case represents a paradigm shift in how cold cases are approached, merging traditional forensic techniques with innovative scientific advancements.

The resolution of notorious cases through forensic evidence has profoundly impacted public perception of justice and the efficacy of law enforcement. Each case serves as a reminder of the intricate relationship between science, morality, and the human psyche. As forensic techniques continue to evolve, they promise to unlock more mysteries of murder while posing new ethical dilemmas. True crime enthusiasts remain captivated by these stories, recognizing that the intersection of forensic science and the human element remains a crucial aspect of understanding murder methods and the motivations behind them.

5

Infamous Serial Killers and Their Techniques

Profiles of Notorious Serial Killers

Understanding the psyche of notorious serial killers offers valuable insights into the motivations and methods behind their gruesome actions. Each profile reveals a complex interplay of psychological issues, environmental factors, and often, a disturbing fascination with death. Serial killers such as Ted Bundy, Jeffrey Dahmer, and John Wayne Gacy exemplify this complexity, showcasing how their distinct backgrounds and experiences shaped their murderous tendencies. For true crime enthusiasts, examining these profiles allows for a deeper comprehension of not just the individuals involved, but also the broader societal implications of their crimes.

Ted Bundy, perhaps one of the most infamous serial killers in American history, was known for his charm and intelligence, traits that belied his violent tendencies. Bundy's modus operandi involved luring young women, often through deception, before abducting and murdering them. His ability to blend in with society and gain the trust of his victims highlights a crucial aspect of many serial killers: the façade of normalcy. Psychological evaluations of Bundy reveal a profound narcissism and a need for control, traits that are often prevalent in other serial killers. The chilling nature of his crimes and his subsequent trial captivated the nation, making him a subject of extensive study within forensic psychology.

Jeffrey Dahmer's profile presents a stark contrast to Bundy's. Dahmer's crimes were characterized not only by murder but also by necrophilia and cannibalism, indicating deeply rooted psychological disturbances. Growing up in a troubled household, Dahmer exhibited signs of sociopathy from an early age. His later crimes reflected a desire to possess and control his victims in the most horrifying ways. The forensic science used in Dahmer's case, including the analysis of his living conditions and the remains of his victims, provided critical insights into the mind of a serial killer. For true crime enthusiasts, Dahmer's case underscores the importance of understanding the psychological and environmental dimensions that contribute to such heinous behavior.

John Wayne Gacy further illustrates the chilling complexity of serial killers. Known as the "Killer Clown," Gacy's double life as a community figure and brutal murderer raises significant questions about perceptions of evil. He targeted young men and boys, employing manipulation and deceit to lure them into his home. Gacy's background as a troubled child with a history of abuse reveals how early trauma can manifest in violent behavior later in life. The legal implications of his crimes, including the landmark trial that followed his arrest, have since influenced how society views and prosecutes serial killers. His case is a reminder of the importance of recognizing the signs of danger, even in seemingly harmless individuals.

The study of these notorious serial killers sheds light on broader cultural perspectives regarding murder methods. From the sensationalized media portrayals to the ethical dilemmas faced by those who study such individuals, the fascination with serial killers poses significant questions. The impact of these criminals extends beyond their immediate victims, influencing societal norms, legal systems, and even popular culture. True crime documentaries often delve into these themes, presenting a nuanced exploration of the killers' lives while grappling with the ethics of depicting such violence. By analyzing these profiles, enthusiasts can better understand not only the killers themselves but also the societal reactions and implications of their heinous acts.

Signature Methods: Patterns of Killers

In the annals of true crime, the signature methods employed by killers reveal not only their psychological profiles but also the broader cultural and historical contexts in which they operate. Signature methods are the unique and often repetitive behaviors exhibited by murderers, serving as their calling cards. These methods can range from the way a victim is chosen to the specific techniques used in the act of killing. By examining these patterns, forensic scientists and criminal psychologists can glean insights into the motivations and emotional states of these individuals, providing critical information for both investigations and legal proceedings.

Historical murder methods have evolved significantly over time, reflecting changes in societal norms, technological advancements, and the legal landscape. For instance, the prevalence of poison as a murder method in the 19th century speaks to both the accessibility of toxic substances and the social dynamics of that era, where clandestine motives often masked the act of killing. Conversely, contemporary killers may utilize firearms or even digital means to execute their crimes, showcasing a shift towards more impersonal methods. These historical patterns not only inform our understanding of specific cases but also highlight broader trends in criminal behavior and societal response to violence.

The psychological profiles of murderers often reveal a complex interplay between their signature methods and underlying mental health issues. Many infamous serial killers exhibit specific patterns that correlate with their psychological disorders, such as narcissism, psychopathy, or trauma-related conditions. For example, Ted Bundy's choice of victims and his method of luring them into vulnerable situations reflect deep-seated issues of control and domination. Understanding these psychological elements is essential for law enforcement agencies, as it aids in profiling and predicting potential future crimes by similar offenders.

Forensic science plays a pivotal role in analyzing signature methods, utilizing cutting-edge technology to connect the dots between crime scenes, victims, and suspects. Advances in DNA analysis, blood spatter pattern analysis, and digital forensics have revolutionized the way investigators approach murder cases. By examining the unique elements of a killer's method, forensic experts can often establish links between seemingly unrelated cases, leading to breakthroughs in investigations. This scientific approach not only enhances the chances of solving cold cases but also contributes to a better understanding of the criminal mind.

Cultural perspectives on murder methods can vary widely, influencing both societal reactions and legal implications. In some cultures, certain methods of killing may be seen through the lens of honor or vengeance, while in others, they may be viewed as abhorrent and unforgivable. This cultural context shapes public perception and can impact the legal proceedings that follow. True crime documentaries often explore these nuances, shedding light on the multifaceted nature of murder methods and the ethical considerations that arise in their study. As enthusiasts delve into these narratives, they uncover the intricate tapestry of human behavior that drives individuals to commit such heinous acts, prompting deeper reflection on morality, justice, and the societal frameworks that influence them.

Impact on Society: Fear and Fascination

The phenomenon of murder evokes a complex interplay of fear and fascination within society, serving as a mirror reflecting our deepest anxieties and morbid curiosities. This duality is evident in the way true crime enthusiasts engage with the subject matter, often captivated by the intricate details of historical murder methods and the psychological profiles of murderers. The darker aspects of human nature are laid bare through the examination of infamous serial killers and their techniques, drawing individuals into a realm where horror coexists with intrigue. This relationship between fear and fascination shapes public perceptions of crime, influencing everything from media representation to cultural narratives surrounding violence.

Fear plays a crucial role in societal reactions to murder, often leading to heightened anxiety about safety and the unpredictability of human behavior. As true crime enthusiasts delve into the intricacies of murder cases, they confront the unsettling reality that the potential for violence exists in everyday life. This awareness can create a sense of vulnerability, prompting discussions about preventive measures, community safety, and the psychological factors that drive individuals to commit heinous acts. The fear of becoming a victim, or the fear of the unknown, serves to bind communities together, often resulting in collective calls for justice and reform in legal implications surrounding various murder methods.

Conversely, fascination with murder often stems from an inherent desire to understand the motives and circumstances that lead to such extreme behaviors. True crime enthusiasts are drawn to the psychological profiles of murderers, seeking to unravel the complexities of their minds. This intellectual pursuit not only satisfies a curiosity about evil but also provides insights into the social conditions that can foster criminal behavior. By analyzing notorious cases and the forensic science involved in solving them, individuals can gain a deeper appreciation for the intricacies of human psychology and the factors that contribute to violent crime.

The portrayal of murder in true crime documentaries and literature further amplifies society's fascination. These narratives often glamorize the act of murder while simultaneously exposing the horror of its realities. They create a safe space for audiences to explore their fears and curiosities vicariously through the stories of others. This exploration can lead to ethical considerations regarding the representation of victims and the glorification of killers, igniting debates about the responsibilities of media creators in their depictions of crime. While some argue that such portrayals can desensitize audiences to violence, others believe they offer valuable lessons about morality and the human condition.

Ultimately, the impact of murder on society is a multifaceted phenomenon characterized by fear and fascination. As true crime enthusiasts navigate this landscape, they contribute to an ongoing dialogue about the nature of violence, the human psyche, and the societal structures that shape our understanding of crime. The study of historical murder methods and unsolved cases fosters a deeper comprehension of these themes, provoking critical thought about the implications of our fascination with the macabre. This engagement not only enriches individual perspectives but also informs broader societal discussions about justice, ethics, and the complexities of human behavior.

6

Cultural Perspectives on Murder Methods

Murder Across Cultures: A Global View

Murder, a universal yet culturally specific phenomenon, manifests in various forms across the globe, shaped by social norms, legal structures, and historical contexts. In examining murder methods from a global perspective, it becomes evident that cultural beliefs and practices significantly influence not only the act itself but also the motivations and justifications behind it. For instance, some cultures may view honor killings as a justified response to perceived slights against family reputation, while others condemn such actions vehemently. These cultural frameworks provide a lens through which to understand the complexities surrounding murder, revealing that what is considered a crime in one society may be sanctioned in another.

Historically, murder methods have evolved alongside societal changes, technological advancements, and shifts in moral standards. In ancient societies, violent acts were often intertwined with rites of passage or expressions of power. The gladiatorial games of Rome and the human sacrifices of the Aztecs illustrate how murder was ritualized and, in some cases, celebrated. As societies developed, so too did the methods and motivations behind murder. The rise of forensic science and legal systems has transformed the landscape, leading to a more systematic approach to understanding and prosecuting such acts. Yet, the historical context of murder remains essential for true crime enthusiasts seeking to comprehend the roots of violent behavior.

Psychological profiles of murderers also vary significantly across different cultures, influenced by local beliefs about mental health, socialization, and crime. In some cultures, mental illness may be stigmatized, leading to a lack of understanding regarding the psychological underpinnings of violent crime. Conversely, other societies may adopt a more empathetic approach, seeking to understand the motivations behind a murder, whether rooted in trauma, societal pressures, or other psychological factors. Serial killers, for instance, often emerge from specific socio-cultural backgrounds, with their methods reflecting the values and taboos of their communities. Analyzing these profiles provides insight into why certain methods are preferred by individuals within particular cultural contexts.

Forensic science plays a pivotal role in murder investigations, yet its application can differ dramatically based on cultural attitudes toward law enforcement and justice. In some regions, technological advancements such as DNA analysis have revolutionized the way murder cases are solved, leading to higher rates of conviction for violent crimes. In contrast, in areas plagued by corruption or a lack of resources, forensic science may be underutilized, resulting in many murder cases remaining unsolved or improperly handled. Documentaries on true crime often highlight these disparities, drawing attention to the systemic issues that affect murder investigations across different cultures and emphasizing the importance of ethical considerations in the portrayal of such cases.

Legal implications surrounding murder methods also reflect cultural attitudes and historical precedents. Some societies impose severe penalties for murder, including capital punishment, while others focus on rehabilitation and restorative justice. The cultural narratives surrounding justice influence public perception and the legal framework within which murder cases are prosecuted. True crime enthusiasts often delve into these legal aspects, analyzing high-profile cases to understand how cultural context shapes judicial outcomes. As such, the study of murder methods transcends mere fascination; it invites a deeper exploration of the societal values, psychological factors, and ethical dilemmas that define humanity's darkest acts.

Ritualistic Killings: The Intersection of Culture and Crime

Ritualistic killings, often steeped in cultural significance, represent a chilling intersection of tradition and violence. Across various societies, these acts are frequently intertwined with spiritual beliefs, societal norms, and communal practices. Such murders are not merely acts of violence but are often seen as fulfilling a deeper purpose, be it religious, sacrificial, or even as a means of asserting power. The motivations behind these killings can vary widely, ranging from the desire to appease deities to the pursuit of personal or political gain, revealing a complex tapestry of human behavior that fascinates true crime enthusiasts.

Historically, ritualistic killings have been documented in numerous cultures, from the Aztecs who practiced human sacrifice to appease their gods, to certain African tribal rituals where sacrifices were believed to ensure good fortune or fertility. The psychological profiles of perpetrators involved in such killings often reveal deep-seated beliefs and a dichotomy between cultural loyalty and moral ethics. These individuals may view their actions as a means of upholding tradition or fulfilling a divine mandate, which complicates the legal implications of their crimes. Understanding these motives provides insight into why such acts can persist in modern society, even in the face of evolving moral standards.

Forensic science plays a crucial role in investigating ritualistic killings, often requiring a multidisciplinary approach that incorporates anthropology, psychology, and criminology. The examination of crime scenes in these cases can reveal specific patterns, symbols, or tools that reflect the cultural context of the act. Forensic experts utilize various techniques, such as trace evidence analysis and psychological profiling, to uncover the motivations behind these gruesome acts. This intersection of culture and crime not only aids in solving cases but also raises ethical considerations about how such methods are portrayed in true crime media, which can sometimes sensationalize the cultural aspects of these killings.

Infamous serial killers have often employed ritualistic elements in their methods, adding layers of intrigue to their criminal profiles. Figures like

Ted Bundy and Jeffrey Dahmer, though not always overtly tied to cultural traditions, incorporated elements of ritual in their approaches, demonstrating how personal pathology can intersect with ritualistic behavior. This melding of individual motivation with cultural practices creates a unique blend of horror that captivates true crime enthusiasts and scholars alike. Analyzing these cases provides valuable insights into the darker aspects of human nature and the potential for cultural influences to shape criminal behavior.

Lastly, the discussion surrounding ritualistic killings invites a broader dialogue about the ethical implications of studying such methods. As true crime enthusiasts delve into these narratives, it is vital to approach them with sensitivity and an awareness of the cultural contexts involved. The portrayal of ritualistic killings in documentaries and literature can perpetuate stereotypes and misunderstandings about the cultures from which they arise. Therefore, it is essential to balance the fascination with these crimes with a respect for the underlying cultural narratives, ensuring that the exploration of ritualistic killings contributes to a deeper understanding rather than a mere sensationalist spectacle.

Media Representation of Murder in Different Cultures

Media representation of murder varies significantly across different cultures, reflecting societal values, historical contexts, and psychological underpinnings. In many Western cultures, media portrayals of murder often sensationalize violence, leading to a morbid fascination with the act itself. Documentaries and dramatizations frequently emphasize the psychological profiles of serial killers, presenting them as enigmatic figures whose motives and methods captivate audiences. This portrayal can sometimes overshadow the victims and the implications of these crimes, leading to a skewed understanding of murder that prioritizes the killer's persona over the societal impact of their actions.

In contrast, Asian media often approaches murder with a more nuanced lens. Traditional narratives may focus on the moral intricacies surrounding murder, often embedding philosophical questions about justice, honor, and retribution. For instance, in Japanese cinema, films often explore the psychological torment of both the murderer and the victim's family, creating a complex emotional landscape that encourages viewers to reflect on the broader implications of violence. Such representations can serve as cautionary tales, prompting discussions about societal issues that may contribute to criminal behavior rather than merely depicting the act itself.

Latin American media frequently intertwines murder with themes of corruption and systemic violence, particularly in the context of drug cartels and organized crime. Telenovelas and crime dramas often depict murder not just as an individual act but as a symptom of larger societal issues, such as poverty and political instability. This representation can foster a sense of collective trauma and urgency within communities, driving home the idea that murder is a societal concern rather than an isolated event. Such portrayals challenge audiences to grapple with the underlying factors that lead to violent crime and highlight the need for systemic change.

African media representations of murder can vary widely, but many narratives emphasize the communal impact of violence. In numerous cultures, storytelling traditions play a crucial role in how murder is understood and discussed. Films and literature often showcase the ripple effects of murder on families and communities, highlighting themes of grief, loss, and resilience. By focusing on the aftermath rather than the act itself, these narratives encourage a deeper understanding of the human experience surrounding violent crime, emphasizing the importance of healing and societal support systems.

The representation of murder in various cultures also raises ethical considerations regarding how these narratives influence public perception and policy. The sensationalism found in some Western media can lead to fear-mongering and stigmatization of mental illness, while more reflective portrayals in other cultures may promote empathy and understanding. True crime enthusiasts must navigate these cultural narratives critically, recognizing the power of media to shape societal attitudes toward murder. Ultimately, understanding the cultural context of murder representation can provide valuable insights into the complexities of human behavior and the societal structures that both contribute to and seek to mitigate violence.

7

Legal Implications of Various Murder Methods

Legal Definitions of Murder

Legal definitions of murder vary significantly across jurisdictions, but they generally share common elements that help distinguish murder from other forms of homicide. At its core, murder is typically defined as the unlawful killing of another human being with malice aforethought. Malice aforethought refers to the intention to kill or cause serious harm, or a depraved indifference to human life. This distinction is crucial in legal contexts, as it

LEGAL IMPLICATIONS OF VARIOUS MURDER METHODS

sets murder apart from manslaughter, which may involve a lack of intent or provocation. Understanding these definitions is essential for true crime enthusiasts seeking to grasp the complexities of legal systems and how they classify different forms of homicide.

In many legal systems, murder is categorized into degrees, primarily first-degree and second-degree murder. First-degree murder is characterized by premeditation, meaning the perpetrator planned the act before carrying it out. This level of intent often results in harsher penalties, including life imprisonment or the death penalty in some jurisdictions. Conversely, second-degree murder lacks the element of premeditation but still involves intent to kill or cause serious injury. Legal definitions also encompass felony murder, where an individual can be charged with murder if a death occurs during the commission of a dangerous felony, regardless of intent to kill.

The legal implications of these definitions are significant, particularly in high-profile murder cases that attract public and media scrutiny. Forensic evidence, such as DNA analysis, can be pivotal in establishing intent and degree of murder. In cases involving notorious serial killers, understanding the legal definitions helps unpack the psychological profiles of these individuals and the motivations behind their crimes. The interplay between forensic science and legal definitions is crucial in building a case, as it can determine whether a charge is upgraded from manslaughter to murder based on the evidence presented.

Cultural perspectives also shape how murder is defined and prosecuted. In some cultures, certain forms of homicide may be viewed through the lens of honor or retribution, influencing legal standards and societal reactions. This cultural context can lead to disparities in how murder is perceived and punished, further complicating the legal landscape. True crime enthusiasts must consider these cultural dimensions when analyzing infamous cases, as they can reveal underlying societal values and the evolution of legal definitions over time.

Lastly, ethical considerations arise in the study of murder methods and their legal ramifications. True crime enthusiasts are often drawn to the gruesome aspects of murder, yet it is vital to approach these topics with sensitivity to the victims and their families. The legal definitions of murder serve not only to categorize acts but also to reflect societal values regarding justice and morality. Engaging with these definitions allows enthusiasts to better understand the broader implications of murder in both historical and contemporary contexts, highlighting the need for a responsible and informed discourse surrounding such a complex topic.

The Death Penalty: A Controversial Method of Justice

The death penalty has long been a contentious issue within the realm of justice, provoking intense debate among legal scholars, ethicists, and the general public. Its roots can be traced back to ancient civilizations, where capital punishment was often employed as a means of retribution or deterrence. Various methods, ranging from hanging to the electric chair, have been utilized throughout history, each reflecting societal values and the prevailing attitudes toward crime and punishment. As true crime enthusiasts delve into the complexities of murder methods, understanding the implications of the death penalty becomes crucial in exploring the broader narratives surrounding justice and morality.

One of the most significant aspects of the death penalty is its psychological impact on both the convicted individuals and society at large. For murderers, the prospect of facing capital punishment can serve as a profound deterrent, yet it can also lead to a sense of fatalism or resignation. This psychological dynamic often plays a role in the profiles of notorious serial killers, many of whom view their crimes as a means of asserting power or control. Analyzing the mindsets of these offenders can provide valuable insights into why some murderers commit heinous acts despite the potential consequences, including the ultimate punishment.

From a forensic science perspective, the death penalty raises numerous legal implications that are critical for true crime enthusiasts to understand. The process of determining guilt in capital cases often involves complex evidentiary standards and the necessity for thorough investigations. Advances in forensic techniques, such as DNA analysis, have transformed the landscape of criminal justice, leading to both convictions and exonerations. Cases of wrongful convictions have ignited fervent debates about the reliability of evidence and the moral responsibility of the state in administering the death penalty, highlighting the potential for irreversible mistakes within the justice system.

Cultural perspectives on the death penalty vary widely across different societies and historical periods, influencing how murder methods are perceived and sanctioned. In some cultures, capital punishment is viewed as a legitimate form of justice, while in others, it is seen as barbaric and inhumane. This divergence often reflects deeper societal values regarding life, death, and the role of punishment in deterring crime. True crime documentaries frequently explore these cultural narratives, presenting a spectrum of viewpoints that deepen the understanding of how justice is administered across the globe.

Ethical considerations surrounding the death penalty continue to fuel ongoing discussions among scholars, legal practitioners, and human rights advocates. The morality of taking a life as punishment remains a divisive issue, with arguments for and against the practice rooted in philosophical, religious, and socio-political beliefs. As true crime enthusiasts engage with these themes, it is essential to consider how the death penalty intersects with broader societal issues, including systemic racism, economic disparity, and the treatment of mental illness in criminal cases. The exploration of these ethical dimensions not only enriches the understanding of murder methods but also prompts critical reflection on the nature of justice itself.

Case Law: Landmark Trials and Their Outcomes

Case law has played a crucial role in shaping the legal landscape surrounding murder, with landmark trials often serving as pivotal moments in both judicial history and public consciousness. These trials have not only influenced legal precedents but have also revealed the complexities of human behavior and societal values. From the courtroom dramas that captivated the nation to the legal ramifications that followed, the outcomes of these cases have had lasting impacts on how murder is prosecuted and understood. By examining significant trials, we can gain insight into the evolving nature of justice and the societal attitudes toward crime and punishment.

One of the most notable trials in American history is the case of the People v. O.J. Simpson, which highlighted the intersection of race, celebrity, and the legal system. The trial, which concluded in 1995, captivated an audience that spanned demographics and raised questions about the efficacy of forensic evidence, the role of media in high-profile cases, and issues of domestic violence. Simpson's acquittal was seen by many as a reflection of broader societal tensions, particularly surrounding race relations in the United States. The trial's outcome not only set a precedent regarding the admissibility of certain types of evidence but also ignited discussions about the fairness of the justice system in cases involving prominent figures.

Another significant trial is that of Ted Bundy, whose heinous acts and subsequent legal proceedings revealed much about the psychological profiles of serial killers. Bundy's trial in the late 1970s was one of the first to extensively utilize forensic psychology in understanding the motivations behind murder. His charm and intelligence complicated public perceptions of evil, challenging the notion that murderers fit a specific mold. The trial's outcome, resulting in Bundy's death penalty sentence, illustrated the legal system's response to particularly egregious acts of violence and set a precedent for how psychological evaluations are considered in murder cases.

The case of the Green River Killer, Gary Ridgway, further emphasizes the legal implications of murder methods and the challenges of prosecuting serial killers. Ridgway's trial in the early 2000s was particularly notable for its use of plea bargaining, which led to his confession to 71 murders in exchange for avoiding the death penalty. This case raised ethical questions regarding the value of confessions obtained through plea deals and the implications for victims' families seeking justice. The legal strategies employed during Ridgway's trial have since influenced how law enforcement approaches similar cases, highlighting the balance between justice and the complexities of legal negotiations in murder cases.

The trials of high-profile murder cases have revealed not only the intricacies of forensic science but also the cultural perspectives that shape societal reactions to crime. Cases such as those of Casey Anthony and Amanda Knox garnered widespread media attention and public scrutiny, reflecting how cultural narratives can influence perceptions of guilt or innocence. The outcomes of these trials demonstrated the potential for societal bias within the legal system and the impact of media portrayal on the judicial process. As true crime enthusiasts delve into these landmark trials, they uncover the multifaceted nature of murder, the psychological profiles of killers, and the ongoing dialogue about morality, justice, and the human condition that continues to evolve through the lens of case law.

8

Murder Methods in True Crime Documentaries

The Popularity of True Crime Documentaries

The popularity of true crime documentaries has surged in recent years, captivating audiences with their intricate storytelling and in-depth exploration of notorious murder cases. This genre appeals to true crime enthusiasts who seek to understand the complexities of criminal behavior, the psychology behind murderers, and the forensic techniques employed in solving these heinous acts.

Documentaries often delve into the historical context of infamous cases, providing viewers with a comprehensive understanding of the societal factors that may contribute to violent crime. The blend of entertainment and education in these films creates a compelling atmosphere for viewers who are eager to learn more about the darker aspects of human nature.

One significant factor contributing to the appeal of true crime documentaries is their ability to present psychological profiles of murderers. By analyzing the motives, backgrounds, and behavioral patterns of criminals, these documentaries provide insights into what drives individuals to commit murder. This exploration of the human psyche not only satisfies a curiosity about the minds of infamous serial killers but also encourages a deeper conversation around mental health and societal influences. Viewers often find themselves reflecting on the thin line between sanity and madness, and the documentaries provoke discussions about the moral implications of understanding such deviant behavior.

Forensic science plays a crucial role in true crime narratives, and documentaries often highlight groundbreaking techniques that have revolutionized criminal investigations. The meticulous process of collecting evidence, analyzing DNA, and employing modern technology is showcased, emphasizing how these advancements have aided law enforcement in solving cold cases and bringing justice to victims. This focus on forensic methods not only educates viewers about the science behind solving murders but also instills a sense of admiration for the professionals dedicated to unraveling these complex cases. Such content resonates with true crime enthusiasts who appreciate the blend of science and law in the pursuit of justice.

Cultural perspectives on murder methods also play a significant role in the popularity of true crime documentaries. Different societies have unique approaches to crime and punishment, influenced by their historical, legal, and cultural contexts. Documentaries often compare and contrast various murder methods across cultures, revealing how societal norms and values shape the way murder is perceived and addressed. This exploration allows viewers to gain a broader understanding of the global implications of violent crime, encouraging them to think critically about the nature of justice and morality in different parts of the world.

Lastly, the ethical considerations surrounding the study of murder methods cannot be overlooked. True crime documentaries often grapple with the morality of sensationalizing real-life tragedies for entertainment purposes. Enthusiasts are frequently urged to reflect on the impact of their consumption habits, considering the victims and families affected by the crimes depicted. Documentaries that approach these topics with sensitivity and respect can foster a deeper understanding and encourage viewers to engage with the material in a thoughtful manner. This ethical dimension enhances the viewing experience, prompting discussions about responsibility and empathy in the context of true crime storytelling.

Case Studies Featured in Documentaries

Case studies featured in documentaries offer a compelling glimpse into the intricacies of murder methods, the profiles of those who commit these heinous acts, and the societal implications surrounding them. Documentaries such as "The Jinx" and "Making a Murderer" delve deep into the psychological landscapes of murderers, unraveling their motivations and the circumstances that led to their criminal behavior. By examining these real-life scenarios, true crime enthusiasts can gain valuable insights into the complex interplay between individual psychology, societal influences, and the methods employed in committing murder.

The portrayal of infamous serial killers in documentaries serves as a crucial educational tool for understanding historical murder methods. For instance, the documentary "Evil Genius" explores the bizarre case of the pizza bomber, revealing not just the method of murder but also the social dynamics and psychological manipulation at play. These case studies highlight how different eras and cultural contexts shape the techniques and motivations behind murder, offering a broader perspective on how societal norms influence criminal behavior.

Forensic science plays a pivotal role in many true crime documentaries, showcasing the evolution of investigative techniques used to solve murder cases. Documentaries like "Forensic Files" illustrate how advancements in DNA analysis and crime scene reconstruction have transformed the landscape of criminal investigations. By featuring real-life cases, these documentaries emphasize the importance of scientific rigor in uncovering the truth behind unsolved murders, shedding light on the legal implications of various murder methods and the challenges faced by law enforcement.

Cultural perspectives on murder methods are also prominently featured in documentaries, revealing how different societies interpret and respond to violent crime. Films such as "The Murder of Laci Peterson" not only detail the crime itself but also explore the media's role in shaping public perception. This cultural lens provides an opportunity for true crime enthusiasts to reflect on how societal values and beliefs influence the understanding of murder, victimhood, and justice, enriching their comprehension of the broader implications of these cases.

Finally, ethical considerations in studying murder methods are an essential aspect of true crime documentaries. While these films aim to educate and inform, they also raise questions about sensationalism and the potential for glorifying criminals. Documentaries such as "The Ted Bundy Tapes" navigate this delicate balance, prompting viewers to consider the moral responsibilities of both the filmmakers and the audience. By critically engaging with these case studies, true crime enthusiasts can better appreciate the complexities surrounding murder and the various factors that contribute to its occurrence, fostering a deeper understanding of this dark facet of human nature.

The Impact of Visual Storytelling on Perception of Murder

Visual storytelling has become an essential tool in shaping the public's perception of murder, particularly in the realm of true crime. Through various mediums such as documentaries, films, and graphic novels, visual narratives create a visceral connection between the audience and the subject matter. These stories often present murder not just as a crime, but as a complex interplay of motives, psychology, and societal implications. By utilizing powerful imagery and compelling narratives, visual storytelling can evoke emotional responses, challenge existing perceptions, and even influence public opinion regarding notorious cases and the methods employed by murderers.

The portrayal of murder methods in visual narratives often emphasizes the sensational aspects of these crimes, which can lead to a distorted understanding of their reality. For instance, true crime documentaries frequently focus on the gruesome details of a murder, highlighting the brutality and drama while glossing over the psychological and sociocultural factors that contribute to such acts. This emphasis on sensationalism can desensitize viewers to the gravity of the crime, reducing complex human behaviors to mere entertainment. As a result, audiences may develop skewed perceptions of not only the methods of murder but also the individuals who commit these acts, often reducing them to archetypal figures rather than fully realized human beings.

Moreover, visual storytelling often employs specific techniques to create a narrative that can sway viewers' sympathies. Filmmakers and authors may choose to focus on the backgrounds of the victims and perpetrators, weaving in elements of their psychological profiles to build a more nuanced understanding. This approach can foster empathy for the victims while simultaneously humanizing the murderers, prompting audiences to consider the underlying factors that drive individuals to commit such heinous acts. The juxtaposition of victim and perpetrator can lead to a more complex dialogue about morality, justice, and the societal conditions that breed violence.

Cultural perspectives on murder methods also play a significant role in how visual storytelling shapes public perception. Different societies have varying attitudes towards violence, justice, and the portrayal of crime. For example, in some cultures, murder may be depicted with a sense of fatalism, while in others, it could be framed as a violation of social norms that demands retribution. These cultural lenses influence the narratives constructed around murder cases, affecting how audiences interpret the actions of both the murderer and the society that fails to prevent the crime. As true crime enthusiasts engage with these narratives, they must navigate the cultural biases embedded within them.

Finally, the ethical considerations surrounding the depiction of murder in visual storytelling cannot be overlooked. As true crime narratives increasingly draw in audiences, there is a responsibility to approach these topics with sensitivity and respect for the real individuals involved. Ethical storytelling encourages a focus on the broader implications of murder, such as its impact on communities and the legal system, rather than merely sensationalizing the acts themselves. By fostering a more thoughtful engagement with the subject, visual storytelling can serve as a powerful medium for deeper understanding, ultimately enriching the discourse surrounding murder methods and their consequences in society.

9

Analysis of Unsolved Murder Cases

Notorious Unsolved Cases

The realm of unsolved murder cases captivates true crime enthusiasts, presenting a unique intersection of mystery and psychological intrigue. Among the most notorious of these cases is the Zodiac Killer, who terrorized Northern California in the late 1960s and early 1970s. Despite the killer's taunting letters and cryptic ciphers sent to newspapers, law enforcement agencies have struggled to identify the perpetrator. This case exemplifies the chilling complexity of psychological profiles, as the Zodiac's calculated evasion of capture and desire for notoriety highlight a deeply troubled mindset, which continues to fascinate criminologists and amateur sleuths alike.

Another infamous unsolved case is that of the Black Dahlia, the gruesome murder of Elizabeth Short in 1947. Found in a vacant lot in Los Angeles, her body was mutilated and displayed with startling precision. The media frenzy that followed not only spotlighted the brutality of the crime but also raised questions regarding the social context of the time, including the cultural perceptions of women and urban crime. This case remains a poignant example of how societal factors can influence public interest in murder methods and the investigative techniques employed by law enforcement, often leading to an enduring legacy of speculation and conspiracy theories.

The disappearance and subsequent murder of the child beauty queen JonBenét Ramsey in 1996 is another case that continues to elude resolution. The tragic and sensationalized nature of her death, combined with the media's relentless scrutiny, has resulted in numerous theories regarding potential suspects, including family members and intruders. The psychological profiles of those involved, including the investigators, have been a focal point for analysis, as the case serves as a cautionary tale about the impact of public perception on criminal investigations. The legal implications of the mishandling of evidence and potential bias have also sparked discussions about the standards of forensic science in high-profile murder cases.

In the realm of serial killers, the case of Jack the Ripper remains one of the most notorious unsolved mysteries in history. Operating in London's Whitechapel district in 1888, the Ripper's brutal methods of murder and mutilation shocked Victorian society. The combination of forensic science advancements and historical documentation allows for ongoing analysis of the killer's psychological profile. Various theories have emerged regarding the identity of Jack the Ripper, with cultural perspectives influencing interpretations of his methods and motivations, further complicating the case's legacy in true crime literature.

Lastly, the unsolved murder of the actress Marilyn Monroe in 1962 continues to fuel speculation and intrigue within the true crime community. While officially ruled a probable overdose, many believe there was foul play involved, possibly linked to her connections with powerful figures. The case highlights the complex relationship between celebrity culture and murder methods, as Monroe's tragic demise has become a subject of numerous documentaries and analyses. Ethical considerations surrounding the portrayal of her death underscore the sensitivity required when discussing unsolved cases, reminding enthusiasts that the narratives we create can have real-world implications on the lives of those left behind.

The Role of Public Interest in Solving Cases

The concept of public interest plays a crucial role in the investigation and resolution of murder cases, influencing both the methods employed by law enforcement and the societal response to crime. In many instances, public opinion can significantly affect the direction of a case, particularly in high-profile murders that capture widespread media attention. This phenomenon can lead to a surge in tips and leads that police might otherwise not receive, as community members feel a personal stake in the resolution of the crime. This collective engagement can act as a double-edged sword; while it can aid in the identification of suspects, it can also create a tumultuous atmosphere where public sentiment may overshadow the legal process.

Moreover, the public's interest often intersects with forensic science, as advancements in technology and techniques can be propelled by societal demands for justice. Cases that draw intense media coverage frequently result in increased funding for forensic investigations, leading to improved methodologies in DNA analysis, ballistics, and digital forensics. As true crime enthusiasts delve into the intricate details of historical murder methods, they may find that the evolution of forensic science is often catalyzed by the need to satisfy public curiosity and demand for accountability in the justice system. This relationship underscores the importance of community involvement in shaping investigative priorities and funding allocations.

In addition to aiding investigations, public interest can also impact the legal implications surrounding murder cases. High-profile trials often attract significant media coverage, which can influence jury selections and the overall atmosphere in which trials unfold. This phenomenon raises ethical considerations about the fairness of legal proceedings, as jurors may be swayed by pre-trial publicity or public opinion. Consequently, legal professionals must navigate the delicate balance between ensuring a fair trial and addressing the public's desire for transparency and information regarding the case.

Cultural perspectives on murder methods can further complicate the role of public interest in solving cases. Different communities may have varying thresholds for what constitutes acceptable violence or justified homicide, which can influence how murder cases are perceived and prosecuted. This cultural lens informs societal expectations and reactions to murder cases, often leading to polarized opinions that can complicate investigations.

ANALYSIS OF UNSOLVED MURDER CASES

Understanding these dynamics is essential for law enforcement and legal professionals, as they must account for the cultural context in which these crimes occur and how public sentiment may affect their work.

Finally, the role of public interest extends into the realm of ethical considerations in studying murder methods. True crime enthusiasts often grapple with the moral implications of dissecting violent acts for entertainment or educational purposes. While the examination of murder cases can lead to a greater understanding of criminal psychology and methods, it is essential to approach these topics with sensitivity to the victims and their families. Engaging with the public responsibly can foster a more informed and compassionate dialogue surrounding crime, ultimately benefiting society as a whole. As the interplay between public interest and the resolution of murder cases continues to evolve, it remains a vital aspect of the ongoing discourse in the field of true crime.

Techniques Used to Reinvestigate Cold Cases

In recent years, the reinvestigation of cold cases has gained momentum, driven by advancements in forensic science and a growing societal interest in unresolved crimes. Techniques employed in these investigations often incorporate a blend of traditional investigative methods and modern technology, creating a comprehensive approach to uncovering the truth behind these long-standing mysteries. Investigators now frequently utilize DNA profiling, which has revolutionized the ability to link suspects to crimes committed decades ago. This technique can analyze even the smallest biological samples, allowing for breakthroughs in cases that once seemed hopeless.

Another critical technique in the reinvestigation of cold cases is the use of digital forensics. With the proliferation of digital devices, law enforcement agencies have harnessed the power of technology to retrieve and analyze information from smartphones, computers, and social media platforms. This data can provide vital insights into a suspect's movements, communications, and connections to the victim. Moreover, investigators often revisit old evidence with new technology, such as enhanced imaging techniques that can reveal details previously obscured, leading to fresh leads and potential breakthroughs in cases that have stymied detectives for years.

Psychological profiling has also evolved as a key tool in the investigation of cold cases. By analyzing the behavior and characteristics of known offenders, investigators can formulate profiles that assist in narrowing down potential suspects. This technique, rooted in the understanding of criminal psychology, allows law enforcement to focus their efforts on individuals who exhibit similar traits or patterns to those of historical offenders. When combined with geographic profiling, which examines the locations of crimes to predict future incidents, the chances of solving cold cases significantly increase.

Collaborative efforts among law enforcement agencies have become increasingly important in tackling cold cases. Many jurisdictions now participate in databases that allow for the sharing of information and leads across state lines. This collaboration extends to partnerships with nonprofit organizations and academic institutions, which can provide additional resources and expertise. Some groups focus on advocating for the reinvestigation of cold cases, drawing public attention and resources to these often-overlooked investigations. This collective approach not only brings fresh eyes to old cases but also fosters a community of support for victims' families seeking closure.

Finally, the ethical considerations surrounding the reinvestigation of cold cases cannot be overlooked. While technology offers powerful tools for solving these cases, it also raises questions about privacy and the potential for wrongful accusations. Investigators must balance the desire for justice with the need to uphold ethical standards and respect for individuals' rights. Engaging with the families of victims and ensuring transparency in the investigative process are crucial steps in maintaining public trust. As techniques continue to evolve, the commitment to ethical practices remains a cornerstone of the reinvestigation process, ensuring that the pursuit of justice does not come at the expense of integrity.

10

Ethical Considerations in Studying Murder Methods

The Morality of Murder Research

The morality of murder research is a complex and often contentious issue that raises profound ethical questions for scholars, criminologists, and true crime enthusiasts alike. At its core, this research seeks to dissect the motivations, methods, and implications of murder, offering insights that can deepen our understanding of human behavior. However, the act of studying murder—especially in its most heinous forms—invites scrutiny over

ETHICAL CONSIDERATIONS IN STUDYING MURDER METHODS

whether such investigations can sometimes glorify or trivialize the very real suffering experienced by victims and their families. This tension between knowledge and ethics is a foundational aspect of the discourse surrounding murder research.

One of the primary concerns in the morality of murder research lies in the potential desensitization of audiences. True crime enthusiasts may find themselves drawn to the sensational aspects of murder methods and infamous serial killers, often leading to a romanticized view of violence. While understanding the psychological profiles of murderers can be crucial in preventing future crimes, it is essential to approach these topics with sensitivity to the victims' narratives. Researchers and writers must navigate the fine line between scholarly inquiry and voyeurism, ensuring that the human cost of murder is neither forgotten nor overshadowed by fascination with the criminal mind.

Furthermore, the cultural perspectives on murder methods can complicate the morality of this research. Different societies have varied historical contexts and legal frameworks surrounding murder, influencing how acts of violence are perceived and studied. Exploring these cultural dimensions can provide valuable insights into the societal factors that contribute to murder, yet it also raises ethical questions about representation and bias. Researchers must be cautious not to impose their own cultural viewpoints when analyzing murder methods across diverse societies, as this could lead to misconceptions and reinforce stereotypes.

The legal implications of studying murder methods also warrant careful consideration. Legal systems often grapple with how to classify and prosecute different forms of murder, each carrying varying degrees of culpability and punishment. This complexity can be reflected in research, where the nuances of each case must be examined with a critical eye. Ethical research should not only seek to document and analyze these methods but also consider how such knowledge can impact public perception and legal proceedings. A responsible approach to murder research involves an awareness of how findings might influence policy and society at large.

In conclusion, the morality of murder research is an essential consideration for those engaged in

ETHICAL CONSIDERATIONS IN STUDYING MURDER METHODS

the study of this dark facet of human behavior. As true crime enthusiasts delve into the intricacies of murder methods and the psychological profiles of killers, it is crucial to maintain an ethical framework that prioritizes the dignity of victims and the potential repercussions of the research on society. Balancing the pursuit of knowledge with ethical responsibility is paramount in ensuring that the study of murder contributes to understanding rather than sensationalism, ultimately fostering a more informed and compassionate discourse around such a tragic aspect of human existence.

The Impact of Sensationalism on Victims' Families

The impact of sensationalism on victims' families is a profound and often overlooked aspect of true crime narratives. Sensationalism, characterized by exaggerated reporting and dramatization, frequently distorts the realities surrounding violent crimes. For the families of victims, this distortion can lead to a painful public spectacle, where grief is overshadowed by media portrayals that prioritize entertainment over empathy. Families may find themselves thrust into the limelight, forced to navigate their trauma while responding to a barrage of sensational headlines and stories that can misrepresent the truth of their loved one's life and death.

Victims' families often grapple with the dual burden of mourning and media scrutiny. As true crime enthusiasts delve into the details of a case, they may inadvertently contribute to this scrutiny, consuming content that is shaped by sensationalist angles. The emotional toll can be immense, as families must contend with the invasive nature of public interest in their tragedy. This scrutiny can lead to a feeling of powerlessness, as the narrative surrounding their loved one is shaped by those who have little understanding of the family's reality, often reducing complex human experiences to mere spectacle.

Furthermore, sensationalism can distort the public's perception of both the victim and the perpetrator, leading to harmful stereotypes and assumptions. Families may feel that the portrayal of their loved ones is simplistic or one-dimensional, often focusing solely on the circumstances of the murder rather than the victim's life, aspirations, and relationships. This focus can perpetuate a narrative that vilifies the perpetrator while simultaneously minimizing the victim's humanity, creating a dangerous cycle of misunderstanding and stigma that affects how families are viewed by society.

In addition to the emotional consequences, there are also legal implications stemming from sensationalized media coverage. Families of victims may face challenges in the pursuit of justice, as sensationalism can influence public opinion and, in some cases, even jury behavior. When the media sensationalizes a case, it can lead to a rush to judgment, impacting the fairness of legal proceedings. Families may feel that their quest for justice is compromised by the very narratives that should be supporting their cause, as sensational coverage can overshadow the facts of the case, complicating legal processes and outcomes.

Ultimately, the impact of sensationalism on victims' families highlights the ethical considerations inherent in the study of murder methods and true crime narratives. True crime enthusiasts must navigate the fine line between fascination with the macabre and respect for the individuals affected by these tragedies. As they explore historical murder methods, psychological profiles, and forensic science, it is crucial to remember the human stories behind the headlines. By fostering a more responsible engagement with true crime narratives, enthusiasts can honor the memories of victims and support their families in their ongoing journeys of healing.

Balancing Education and Ethics in True Crime

Balancing education and ethics in the realm of true crime is a critical endeavor, especially when delving into the darker aspects of human behavior. The study of murder methods and the psychological profiles of murderers can provide valuable insights into criminal behavior, but it also raises significant ethical considerations. True crime enthusiasts must navigate the fine line between educating themselves about these subjects and engaging in sensationalism that can exploit victims and their families. The goal should be to foster a deeper understanding of the complexities surrounding murder while maintaining respect for those affected by such tragedies.

Historical murder methods offer a fascinating glimpse into the evolution of criminal behavior and societal responses to violence. However, discussing these methods requires a thoughtful approach. Enthusiasts should strive to contextualize historical cases within their societal frameworks rather than glorifying the perpetrators. This contextualization not only enhances educational value but also helps to humanize the victims, reminding audiences that behind every case is a real person whose life was irrevocably altered or lost. By emphasizing the historical and cultural contexts of murder methods, true crime enthusiasts can promote a more nuanced understanding of these issues.

The psychological profiles of infamous serial killers reveal patterns and motivations that are crucial for forensic science and criminal psychology. Yet, when analyzing these profiles, it is essential to consider the ethical implications of labeling individuals as "monsters." Such terminology can dehumanize both the perpetrator and the victim, leading to a dangerous narrative that oversimplifies complex human behaviors. True crime enthusiasts should be mindful of the language they use and strive to present psychological analyses that prioritize empathy and understanding over sensationalism. This balanced approach not only educates audiences but also fosters a more compassionate discourse around crime and punishment.

The portrayal of murder methods in true crime documentaries often straddles the line between education and exploitation. While these documentaries can serve as informative resources, they can also sensationalize violence, thereby desensitizing viewers to the real-life implications of murder. True crime enthusiasts must critically evaluate the content they consume and support media that prioritizes ethical storytelling. Documentaries that honor the victims and provide a comprehensive look at the factors surrounding the crimes can contribute positively to public understanding while avoiding the pitfalls of glorifying violence.

ETHICAL CONSIDERATIONS IN STUDYING MURDER METHODS

Lastly, the legal implications of various murder methods present another layer of complexity in the discussion of education and ethics. Legal outcomes are often influenced by societal perceptions of crime, which can be shaped by true crime narratives. This interplay highlights the responsibility of true crime enthusiasts to advocate for informed discussions about justice, prevention, and rehabilitation. By engaging with these topics thoughtfully, enthusiasts can contribute to a more educated public discourse that respects the intricacies of the legal system while promoting ethical considerations in the study of murder methods. Balancing education and ethics in true crime is not merely a challenge; it is an opportunity to enrich understanding while honoring the humanity of all involved.

11

Conclusion

Reflections on the Journey Through Murder Methods

The study of murder methods throughout history reveals a complex tapestry woven from societal influences, psychological profiles, and forensic advancements. Each method reflects not just the act of taking a life but also the cultural and historical contexts in which these acts were committed. From the brutal simplicity of bludgeoning to the calculated precision of poisoning, the evolution of murder techniques provides insights into the human psyche and societal norms. True crime enthusiasts are drawn to these narratives, seeking to understand the motivations behind such heinous acts and the implications they hold for justice and society.

Delving into historical murder methods allows us to appreciate the changing landscape of crime and punishment. In ancient times, methods were often public and brutal, serving as a warning to others. As societies evolved, the means of murder became more sophisticated, reflecting advancements in technology and shifts in moral perspectives. The infamous Jack the Ripper case exemplifies this transition, where the method was not only a reflection of the killer's psychological state but also a commentary on the social issues of Victorian London. Each case serves as a historical snapshot, revealing how murder methods can serve as a mirror to the era's values and fears.

Psychological profiles of murderers provide an essential layer of understanding in the study of murder methods. The motivations behind different techniques—be it passion, revenge, or a desire for power—are often tied to the murderer's background and mental state. Serial killers, in particular, exhibit distinct patterns in their methods, which can often be traced back to their upbringing, trauma, or psychological disorders. By analyzing these profiles, enthusiasts can gain insights into the motivations that drive individuals to commit such acts, which in turn informs the broader discourse on criminal behavior and prevention strategies.

Forensic science has revolutionized how murder cases are investigated and understood. The application of forensic techniques not only aids in solving crimes but also shapes public perceptions of murder methods. Advances in DNA analysis, ballistics, and toxicology have made it possible to dissect murder methods with unprecedented accuracy. True crime documentaries often highlight these breakthroughs, showcasing how forensic evidence can unravel the complexities of a case. This intersection of science and crime captivates audiences, as they witness the unfolding of a narrative that combines human ingenuity with the darker aspects of human nature.

Ethical considerations play a crucial role in the study of murder methods, particularly as true crime continues to gain popularity. As enthusiasts engage with these narratives, it is essential to balance the fascination with the gravity of the subject matter. The portrayal of murder methods in media can sometimes sensationalize violence or trivialize the experiences of victims and their families. Ethical engagement with these topics demands a critical approach, encouraging a respectful dialogue that acknowledges the real human suffering behind the statistics and stories. This reflection on the journey through murder methods not only enhances our understanding but also fosters a responsible and informed discourse among true crime enthusiasts.

The Future of Murder Studies and True Crime

The future of murder studies and true crime is poised for significant evolution, driven by advancements in technology, shifts in societal attitudes, and an ever-growing interest in psychological profiling. As forensic science continues to develop, new methodologies such as advanced DNA analysis and digital forensics are expected to enhance our understanding of historical murder methods and their implications. These advancements will not only aid in solving cold cases but also provide deeper insights into the psychological profiles of murderers, allowing researchers and enthusiasts alike to dissect the motivations and circumstances surrounding infamous serial killers and their techniques.

In addition to technological advancements, the cultural perspectives on murder methods are likely to shift as societies grapple with issues such as mental health, social justice, and the portrayal of violence in media. True crime documentaries and podcasts have surged in popularity, often sparking discussions about the ethics of sensationalizing real-life tragedies. This cultural scrutiny will lead to a more nuanced exploration of murder, encouraging scholars and enthusiasts to consider the broader societal contexts that contribute to violent behavior. Future studies will likely emphasize the importance of understanding murder within its cultural framework rather than simply categorizing it as a series of heinous acts.

The legal implications of various murder methods will also play a crucial role in future discussions. As laws evolve in response to changing societal norms and scientific advancements, there will be greater emphasis on how legal systems address different murder methods, including premeditated versus impulsive acts. This shift will compel researchers to analyze the effectiveness of current legal frameworks in dealing with murder cases, particularly in the context of emerging forensic evidence. The interaction between law and forensic science will become increasingly central to discussions about accountability and justice in murder cases.

Furthermore, the growing interest in analyzing unsolved murder cases will likely inspire a new generation of true crime enthusiasts and scholars. These cases often serve as a reflection of societal fears and unresolved issues, compelling the public to engage with the complexities of murder in a more profound way. As forensic techniques improve, opportunities for re-examining cold cases will abound, prompting fresh analyses and possibly leading to breakthroughs that have eluded investigators for decades. This pursuit will not only satisfy curiosity but also highlight the importance of ongoing research into unsolved cases as a means of preventing future violence.

Lastly, ethical considerations in studying murder methods will remain a critical aspect of future true crime discourse. As society continues to confront the moral ramifications of depicting real-life violence, discussions will become more robust regarding the responsibilities of creators and scholars in the field. Balancing the fascination with murder and its methods against the need for sensitivity towards victims and their families will be paramount. True crime enthusiasts will need to navigate these ethical waters carefully, ensuring that their passion for understanding murder does not overshadow the human stories behind the statistics, thereby fostering a more respectful and informed dialogue within the community.